How do we know Summer?

Molly Aloian

 Crabtree Publishing Company
www.crabtreebooks.com

Author
Molly Aloian

Publishing plan research and development
Sean Charlebois, Reagan Miller
Crabtree Publishing Company

Editorial director
Kathy Middleton

Editors
Adrianna Morganelli
Crystal Sikkens

Design
Samara Parent
Margaret Amy Salter

Photo research
Samara Parent

**Production coordinator
and prepress technician**
Margaret Amy Salter

Print coordinator
Katherine Berti

Illustrations
Katherine Berti: page 6

Photographs
Thinkstock: page 15 (top)
Wikimedia Commons: ForestWander: page 13
All other images by Shutterstock

Library and Archives Canada Cataloguing in Publication

Aloian, Molly
How do we know it is summer? / Molly Aloian.

(Seasons close-up)
Includes index.
Issued also in electronic formats.
ISBN 978-0-7787-0960-2 (bound).--ISBN 978-0-7787-0964-0 (pbk.)

1. Summer--Juvenile literature. 2. Seasons--Juvenile literature.
I. Title. II. Series: Seasons close-up

QB637.6.A56 2013   j508.2   C2012-907338-5

Library of Congress Cataloging-in-Publication Data

CIP available at Library of Congress

Crabtree Publishing Company

Printed in Hong Kong/012013/BK20121102

www.crabtreebooks.com   1-800-387-7650

Published in Canada
Crabtree Publishing
616 Welland Ave.
St. Catharines, Ontario
L2M 5V6

Published in the United States
Crabtree Publishing
PMB 59051
350 Fifth Avenue, 59th Floor
New York, New York 10118

Published in the United Kingdom
Crabtree Publishing
Maritime House
Basin Road North, Hove
BN41 1WR

Published in Australia
Crabtree Publishing
3 Charles Street
Coburg North
VIC 3058

Contents

What is summer?

Summer is one of the four **seasons** of the year. It always comes after spring. The seasons repeat the same pattern each year. Spring comes before summer, summer changes to fall, fall changes to winter, and winter turns back to spring.

Summer brings a lot of sunlight, so flowers are in full **bloom**.

Feeling hot

Summer is the hottest season of the year. People usually spend a lot of time outside. When people go outside, they must wear light clothing, such as shorts and T-shirts. What do you wear when you go outside to play on a hot summer day?

Why do we have summer?

It takes Earth one year to travel around the Sun. Earth is tilted slightly as its moving. This causes parts of Earth to receive more sunlight at different times of the year. The different amounts of sunlight changes the seasons.

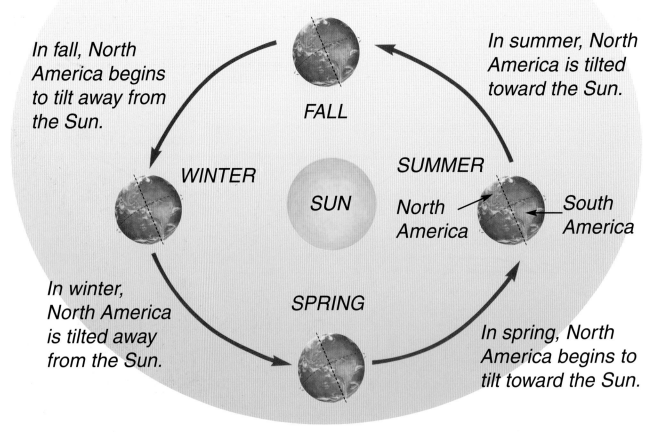

In fall, North America begins to tilt away from the Sun.

In summer, North America is tilted toward the Sun.

FALL

WINTER

SUMMER

SUN

North America

South America

SPRING

In winter, North America is tilted away from the Sun.

In spring, North America begins to tilt toward the Sun.

Tilted toward

During summer in North America, the northern parts of Earth are tilted toward the Sun. They are getting hot **temperatures** and more daylight hours. The southern parts, such as South America, are tilted away from the Sun. This means they are getting cold temperatures and less hours of daylight.

What do you think?

Hot weather and plenty of sunshine are signs that summer has arrived. Can you think of some other signs of summer?

7

When is summer?

In North America, the first day of summer is in June. All the seasons, including summer, last for three months. During summer, the Sun rises early and sets late, so the days are long. Warm nights are a sign that summer has arrived.

Different times

The northern and southern parts of Earth have their seasons at opposite times of the year. For example, in South America, summer starts in December and ends in March. In some parts of the world, there are only two seasons—the wet season and the dry season.

What do you **think?**

During the wet season, there is heavy rain. During the dry season, there is very little rain. Can you tell what season it is in this picture?

Summer weather

Summer weather is hot and sunny. On hot summer days, the Sun is strong and high in the sky. In some places in North America, summer temperatures can reach as high as 100°F (37.8°C).

What do you think?

What do you do to keep cool in the summer?

Hot and sticky

Summer weather is usually dry, but there are sometimes thunderstorms. During thunderstorms, there is heavy rain, thunder, and lightning. Summer weather can also be very **humid**. The air feels hot and sticky. There is no breeze to keep you cool.

Plants in summer

In summer, plants grow quickly. Trees and other plants have plenty of bright green leaves. There are many brightly colored flowers in parks and gardens. What kinds of flowers do you see in summer?

Making seeds

Flowers are different colors, sizes, shapes, and scents. The scents and bright colors of flowers attract insects. Insects land on flowers and carry **pollen** to other flowers. Flowers use pollen to create **seeds**.

This bee has pollen on its body that it will carry from one flower to another.

poller.

13

Animals in summer

In summer, there are animals everywhere. Many baby animals are born in the spring. By the summer, they are ready to start looking for food with their mothers. Some animals, including mice and foxes, stay underground in cool **burrows** during the hottest parts of the day. They search for food at night.

What do you think?

Can you think of some animals you see during the day in the summer?

These Canadian geese babies are out looking for food with their parents.

Sights and sounds of summer

Birds sing songs and splash in water on hot summer days. You might hear bees buzzing or frogs croaking. Crickets make chirping sounds. You may also see fireflies lighting up a summer night.

firefly

This bird is staying cool in the summer heat.

Summer foods

What do you **think?**

Blossoms on apple trees turn into fruit in the summer. What other kinds of fruits grow on trees in summer?

Certain food crops, such as corn and wheat, grow quickly in summer. In late summer or early fall, farmers **harvest** these crops. Many fruits and vegetables also grow in summer. People pick sweet and juicy strawberries, watermelons, and peaches. They also pick bright red tomatoes and crisp, cool cucumbers.

16

I'm melting!

Many people enjoy eating frozen popsicles and ice cream cones on hot summer days. Popsicles and ice cream cones help keep us cool, but they usually melt quickly in the hot summer weather.

Summer fun

School usually ends at the start of summer so many families go on vacation. Some kids go to summer camp. Many people have barbecues in their backyards or go to parks for picnics. It is fun to eat outside during summer.

This family is eating watermelon on their camping trip.

Getting wet

Other summer activities include swimming, going to the beach, visiting splash pads and water parks, and running through sprinklers. You can even splash in water from the hose.

sprinkler

Keeping cool

Many people use fans or **air conditioners** to stay cool in summer. People use fans to create a breeze during hot, calm summer weather. Air conditioners blow cool air into homes and other buildings.

Sitting in the shade will help keep you cool in summer.

Cool clothes

Wearing light clothing also helps keep us cool during hot summer weather. People wear T-shirts, shorts, sandals, and flip-flops. Many people wear hats to protect their heads from the hot Sun. Putting on sunscreen will stop your skin from burning when you are outside.

What do you think?

Think of the clothes you wear in summer. What do summer clothes all have in common?

Sun studies

This activity will help give you a better understanding of the Sun and how it heats the air, land, and water around you. You will need:

Two pans filled with water

Place one pan of water outside in the Sun. Place the other pan of water indoors. After about ten minutes, go outside and stick your fingers in the pan of water.

Is the water hot, warm, or cool? Imagine that the pan was filled with soil or sand. How would the soil or sand feel? Think what the sand feels like at the beach in the summer. Record your answers.

Now go indoors and stick your fingers in the pan of water.

Is the water hot, warm, or cool? Imagine that this pan was filled with soil or sand. How would the soil or sand feel? Why? Record your answers.

Learning more

Books

Exploring Summer (Pebble Plus) by Terri DeGezelle.
  Capstone Press, 2012.
What Is Weather? (Weather Close-Up) by Robin Johnson.
  Crabtree Publishing Company, 2012
Which Season Is It? (My World). by Bobbie Kalman
  Crabtree Publishing Company, 2011
Why Is It Summer? (Why Do We Have Seasons?) by Sara L. Latta.
  Enslow Elementary, 2012.

Websites

Changing Seasons – Exploring Nature Educational Resource
www.exploringnature.org/db/detail.php?dbID=112&detID=2634

Science projects: ideas, topics, methods, and examples
www.sciencemadesimple.com/

The Seasons
http://csep10.phys.utk.edu/astr161/lect/time/seasons.html

Seasons – Science for Kids!
www.historyforkids.org/scienceforkids/physics/weather/seasons.htm

Words to know

air conditioners (AIR kuhn-DISH-uh-ner) noun A machine that cools the temperature of an area by blowing cold air

bloom (BLOOM) noun When the buds of flowers are fully open

burrow (BUR-oh) noun A hole in the ground made by animals

harvest (HAHR-vist) verb To gather or collect a crop

humid (HYOO-mid) adjective Describing air that has a lot of water in it and feels damp

pollen (POL-uhn) noun Tiny, powdery particles in flowers that allow plants to make seeds

season (SEE-zuhn) noun A period of time with certain temperatures and weather

seed (SEED) noun The part of an adult plant that will grow into new plants

temperature (TEHM-per-a-chur) noun How cold or hot the air is

A noun is a person, place, or thing. A verb is an action word that tells you what someone or something does. An adjective is a word that tells you what something is like.

Index

24